Dedication

Charleston, South Carolina is a magnificent city which continuously changes yet preserves the uniqueness of its original southern charm. The skyline changes with new bridges and infrastructure built to accommodate business and pleasure travelers while beautiful parks subtly add enjoyment for both children and adults. By contrast, the beauty of East Bay Street, the charm of Church Street, and the nobility of South Battery are truly captured in time and are a tribute to the city's outstanding job of preservation.

This book is dedicated to the continual preservation of Charleston—the peninsula, the surrounding islands and rivers and especially, our very own "Low Country Hospitality." Without any of these, Charleston would be any other city. Yet, this is Charleston.

Sincerely,

Bryan Riggs

© 1993 Charleston Postcard Company
2136 Coker Avenue
Charleston, SC 29412
Printed in Korea

Photography by Bryan Riggs

ISBN 1-56944-007-7 (Soft Cover)
ISBN 1-56944-008-5 (Hard Cover)

Published by Terrell Publishing Company 1292206
Account Executive—Sean Van Dyne
Art Direction and Design—Dean Eichler
Copy by Susan Trudeau

Table of Contents

HISTORIC HOMES
CHARLESTON • SOUTH CAROLINA

South Battery

Charleston was founded in 1670 and is the oldest city between Virginia and Florida. It was the first capital of the Carolinas and of South Carolina. The young settlement on the west bank of the Ashley River was named Charles Town for King Charles I of England. Charles II granted a charter for a vast area of this new country and called it Carolina, a derivative of Carolus, Latin for Charles, to honor himself. In 1672, plantation owners Henry Hughes and John Coming donated half their land on Oyster Point between the Ashley and Cooper Rivers and the city was relocated across the Ashley River to the Charleston peninsula. The "Grand Modell," a plan of the "New Charles Town" designed by Lord Ashley Cooper, specified lot sizes and street widths. It was drawn to "avoid the undecent and incommodious irregularities which other English colonies are fallen into for want of an early care in laying out the Townes."

Originally called Fort Street, South Battery was a narrow bit of a street running between Church Street and Meeting Street. Today, its historic houses face the site of Ft. Sumter in the distant harbor, where the War Between the States began.

South Battery

Much of Charleston's early prosperity was built on Indian trade, rice, indigo and shipping. Softly tanned deerskins were in high demand for breeches and hats. Experimentally planted rice and indigo became major cash and export crops in the 1730's and 40's. Many of Charleston's merchants soon amassed some of the largest private fortunes of America's Colonial period. Many homes constructed in this period served as places of business as well as dwellings, the second and third floors reserved for family, the main floor for business. The prosperity of their owners was reflected in grand architectural designs.

The exterior of *32 South Battery* features a prominent cupola and a two tiered piazza. The interior is graced with Regency period detailing. The home is believed to have been built for Col. John Ashe in 1782 by a Mr. Miller, credited with design and construction of a number of Charleston's fine homes during that era.

30 South Battery was built in 1860 by James E. Spear. The three story residence is a fine example of Italianate architecture, adapted to the sub-tropical climate of the Carolinas through the addition of piazzas, or shaded porches.

Most of Charleston's elegantly massive homes sit shoulder to shoulder on tiny lots, a carry-over from the crowded European lifestyle the settlers left behind.

32 South Battery

30 South Battery

South Battery

*T*HE beautiful homes along South Battery are an elegant mixture of architectural designs. *20 South Battery* was built in 1843 by Samuel N. Stevens, a prosperous factor. It was remodeled and enlarged in 1870 in Second Empire style for Col. Richard Lathers, a millionaire cotton broker, banker, insurance executive and railroad director, who later served in the Union Army. After the war, Lathers wined and dined military and political leaders at the mansion in an effort to reconcile the nation. His attempts failed. In 1874 he sold the residence to Andrew Simonds, a local banker, and moved North.

22 South Battery, Italianate in design, was built in 1858 for Nathaniel Russell Middleton, a planter.

The home at *24 South Battery* is the western half of an 18th Century double tenement. The eastern half was torn down to accommodate Middleton's home. The building was remodeled in 1870.

The Georgian style home at *8 South Battery* was built in 1768 by Thomas Savage. It was later purchased by Col. William Washington, kinsman of George Washington.

The Italian Villa style mansion at *26 South Battery* was built in 1853 for Col. John Algernon Sydney Ashe. The home features arcades and bracketed cornices.

The home at *28 South Battery* is a stuccoed brick villa built by George S. Cook, the noted photographer, in 1860.

20 South Battery

24 · 22 South Battery

20 South Battery

26 South Battery

8 South Battery

28 South Battery

South Battery

$\mathcal{F}$OUR *South Battery*, an Italian Renaissance Revival style design of F.P. Dinkelberg of New York, was built in 1892-93 by Maj. Andrew Simonds, president of the First National Bank and commodore of the Carolina Yacht Club, for his young bride. In 1909 it became, for a time, the hotel Villa Margherita.

The Stucco house at *2 South Battery* dates from 1905 and was built for the O'Neill sisters. The rear portion encompasses the carriage house of 1 East Battery.

The Magwood-Moreland House at *39 South Battery* was built in 1827. Whether by design or chance, it was built on a foundation of crisscrossed palmetto poles. Some claim the builder intentionally designed the home to be hurricane proof. Others believe the home was constructed atop the remains of a palmetto log fort. Whichever story is accurate, the palmetto foundation allows the house to sway slightly, making it virtually earthquake proof. It was among the homes that survived the 1886 earthquake that leveled most of Charleston. Residents of the Magwood-Moreland home today claim they can still feel a slight sway during gale or hurricane force winds, a testament to the quality and creativity that went into the marvelous homes of this era.

4 South Battery

2 South Battery

39 South Battery

South Battery

Fourty-nine South Battery is believed to have been constructed in 1795 by Col. James English and was occupied by several generations of his descendants. The home is a classic example of the single house style, a unique Charleston design consisting of a house one room wide and two deep, with the narrow end facing the street. A one or two story piazza, designed to catch the cooling sea breezes, was usually added to the side of this type of home. Like many Charleston homes, the entry does not open directly into the house but onto the piazza.

The piazza, as defined by Samuel Johnson in 1750, is "a walk under a roof supported by pillars." Like much of the city's plans and architecture, it is borrowed directly from England. The first piazza was built by architect Inigo Jones at Covent Garden in London. Not only offering a bit of much needed shade to Charleston's homes, the piazza also provided an intimate view of the city's street life. Both airy and functional, the piazza gave builders the opportunity to add graceful columns, capitals and fancy woodwork to the face of otherwise rather austere structures. Unusually, both *44 and 46 South Battery* turn their delightful double piazzas to the street.

49 South Battery

49 South Battery

46 South Battery

44 South Battery

South Battery

*M*ost of Charleston's homes were constructed either very near or right up against the sidewalk line, allowing for little or no room for plantings. The side or rear yards of the homes, artistically fenced, became sheltered and wonderfully lush flower and herb gardens. These gardens were tended by the ladies of the house, usually with the assistance of household slaves.

The house at *56 South Battery* is believed to be of post-revolutionary construction. It has since been remodeled featuring an elegant ironwork second floor piazza. Intricately styled hand wrought iron was used to provide gates, fences and balustrades for many of Charleston's Colonial period homes. Much of this craftsmanship was lost in the 1886 earthquake but enough survived to inspire artisans in the Nineteenth century when cast iron was added to hand wrought work.

During 1984 and 1985, the house and garden at *58 South Battery*, built in 1800 for John Black, was completely restored. Using original diagrams, wrought iron gates, and bricks excavated from the yard, the garden was reconstructed to its splendid beauty.

William Gibbes built *64 South Battery* sometime between 1772 and 1788. A merchant, shipowner and planter, he built a large wharf in front of the house. The gardens were designed by Mrs. Washington A. Roebling, whose husband along with his father, John August Roebling, designed and built the Brooklyn Bridge in 1869-83.

74 South Battery

95 South Battery

56 South Battery

64 South Battery

58 South Battery

Murray Blvd.

Murray Boulevard was named for Andrew Buist Murray, an orphan who became a successful businessman and philanthropist as well as a Charleston benefactor. The 47 acres behind this waterfront boulevard are reclaimed mud flats developed into building lots in 1911. Murray also proposed lengthening East Battery to connect with the boulevard by extending the seawall south of White Point Gardens. This created a lovely riverside boulevard over a mile in length. Murray, at no profit to himself, contributed nearly 50% of the cost of the development.

In the Eighteenth and early Nineteenth centuries, builders lavished a great deal of care, craftsmanship and attention to detail on the staircases, porticos and doorways of Charleston's homes. The double-curving stairs of *28 Murray* and semi-circular pillared entrances of it and *46 Murray* reflect the refined tastes of their first owners. Another sign of wealth and good taste was the addition of massive columns to support and accent the piazzas and entrances as seen in several Murray Boulevard homes. Columns were often topped with ornate establature in Roman or Greek styles.

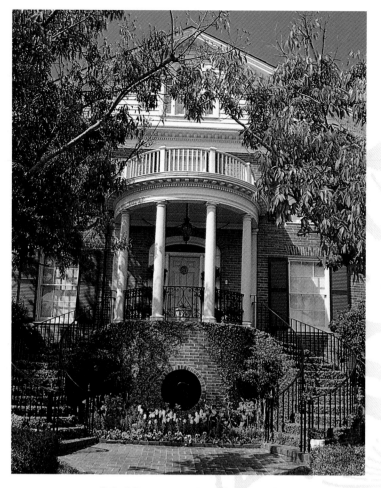

28 Murray Boulevard

46 Murray Boulevard

36 Murray Boulevard

32 Murray Boulevard

Murray Blvd.

$\mathscr{T}$HE home at *52 Murray* was the first to be built on the new boulevard. The imposing Colonial Revival residence was built by C. Bissel Jenkins, one of the pioneers of the Reclamation Movement. The 15 room home, built of Summerville brick with red Ludovici tile roofing, was designed by Walker & Burden Architects. It did not stand alone long and was soon joined by other imposing structures featuring the architectural styles popular in the early 1900's. By the mid-1900's Murray Boulevard bore no resemblance to the area at nearby White Point where famous pirate of the high seas Stede Bonnet was hanged.

In 1718, Edward Teach, alias Blackbeard, arrived off the coast of Charleston with a fleet of pirate ships. His buccaneers seized several merchant ships, capturing, among others Councilman Samuel Wragg and his son. The prisoners were held for ransom. Teach was captured and executed by Virginia authorities. The residents of Charleston did achieve some measure of revenge, however, when Col. William Rhett captured the cut-throat Bonnet and his men in the Cape Fear River. They were tried before Justice Nicholas Trott and hanged on White Point. The bodies were buried below the high water mark on the point.

74 Murray Boulevard

62 Murray Boulevard

46 Murray Boulevard

52 Murray Boulevard

Church St.

℃HURCH Street, named for St. Philip's Church, was part of the original "Grand Modell" for Charles Town in 1672. The houses that continue to stand on Church Street exemplify over three centuries of Charleston's history. *41 Church*, as legend would have it, was built in 1909 on a wager. Architect A.W. Todd was bet that he could not build a respectably large dwelling on a narrow 25 by 150 foot lot - a bet he handily won. An interesting feature of the lovely home is the garage entrance built through the chimney.

39 Church was built nearly two centuries earlier, in 1743 for George Eveleigh. The two and one-half story stuccoed house is built of small bricks and follows an asymmetrical floor plan, popular in early houses. A tornado in 1811 tore away a 30 foot roof beam and drove it into the roof of a house on King Street a quarter of a mile away. The house also once had a secret staircase leading from a cupboard in the drawing room to the closet in a room below, perhaps a lifesaving feature in revolutionary times.

32 Church was built by Robert Lindsay, a carpenter, in the early 1800's.

41 Church St.

39 Church St.

30 Church St.

32 Church St.

31 Church St.

Church St.

THE entrance to 55 *Church* is another example of the fine workmanship and eye for detail that went into creating inviting entrances to the lovely homes on Charleston's streets.

71 Church, of three story stuccoed brick construction, is one of the earliest surviving examples of Charleston single houses. It was built by Col. Robert Brewton perhaps as early as 1721. Brewton was the son of Col. Miles Brewton who fought in the war against the Yemassee Indians in 1715. Col. Robert Brewton was a wealthy wharf owner, a militia officer and a member of the Commons House of Assembly.

59 Church was built by Thomas Rose, an Ashley River planter in 1733, soon after his marriage. It is said the house is haunted by the ghost of Dr. Joseph Brown Ladd who died in a duel defending the honor of a traveling actress nicknamed "Perdita." Mortally wounded by his one time friend Ralph Isaacs, Dr. Ladd died in the house three weeks later, long after the lady in question had left town.

69 Church is a classic example of the double house, almost literally two single houses built together creating a nearly square structure with a room in each corner and a central hall or side hall with a grand staircase, often visible from the front door. The house's ancestry is clouded but it may have been built in 1745 by Richard Capers, a planter, for his third wife. The only public record of the house indicates that Jacob Motte, the Public Treasurer, leased the house from 1761 until his death in 1770.

55 Church Street

71 Church Street

59 Church Street

69 Church Street

Church St.

THE Georgian brick house at *87 Church* was built in 1772 by Daniel Heyward, a rice planter, for his son Thomas, a British-educated attorney, patriot and signer of the Declaration of Independence. In 1791 President George Washington stayed here while visiting the city. In 1794, John Grimke purchased the house. Two of Grimke's daughters later played an active role in the abolitionist movement. Owned by The Charleston Museum, the house is open to the public.

The house at *78 Church* was combined with *76* to create one dwelling. It was in *76 Church* that DuBose Heyward wrote "Porgy," the novel which became the wildly popular operetta "Porgy and Bess." It is believed that President George Washington spoke to the people of Charleston from the balcony of *78 Church* when he visited the city in 1791. The present balcony, however, is in the Regency style of 1815-25. An antique mahogany bedpost partially supports the third floor of this home, proof of the ingenuity of Charleston's residents in overcoming the adversity and hard times that besieged the city after the Revolution.

87 Church Street

74 Church Street

78 Church Street

Church St.

NINETY-TWO *Church* is a three and one half story brick Adamesque home built in 1805 by Alexander Christie, a Scots merchant. The land on which it sits was once the garden of *94 Church*. The middle window on the first floor was originally a door, allowing the room within to be used for business while the family dwelt upstairs. Since 1908 it has been the rectory of St. Philip's Church.

The dwelling at *90 Church* is thought to have been built by Thomas Legare sometime after 1752. Three and one-half stories tall, the brick building is in the Georgian style and features a Regency piazza added in 1816 by George Macaulay. The middle window in the first level was a door. The main floor was probably used as a shop or counting house.

89-91 Church is a three story double tenement building of stuccoed brick dubbed "Cabbage Row" because early 1900's inhabitants set up vegetable stands on the sidewalks. The buildings are the legendary site of DuBose Heyward's "Catfish Row" of "Porgy," patterned after a heart-rending crippled black beggar, "Goat Cart Sammy" Smalls. Smalls and his goat cart begged coins on Charleston's Streets until shortly after World War I. Police records indicate the colorful character shot or shot at many women in his day. In the end, Sammy returned to his wife, Normie, not Bess, on "Jim" Island where he is buried "Crossways of the world" (North-South rather than the customary East-West, because he died as he lived, unrepentant).

92 Church Street

90 Church Street

89 · 91 Church Street

Church St.

NINETY-FOUR Church, a three story hipped roof house, was built between 1760 and 1765 by John Cooper, a leader in the Colonial government and a patriot of the Revolution. From 1771 to 1799, Thomas Bee, an attorney, planter, delegate to the Continental Congress and U.S. Judge, owned the home. It has been mistakenly reported that Mr. Bee built the house in 1730. Gov. Joseph Alston, who was married to Theodosia Burr, daughter of Aaron Burr, Vice President of the United States under Thomas Jefferson, came into ownership a few years later. In 1832, the house was the site chosen by organizers of the Nullification Movement. The movement was designed to establish South Carolina as a sovereign, self governing state, and to nullify the unpopular Tariff Act of 1828. The Act led to the bloody Civil War during which the the Alexander Christie family owned the home.

93 and 95 Church are part of Church Street's later, and quieter history. Built in 1910 on the site of the Charleston Hydraulic Cotton Press Company, these two homes are examples of a row of two and one-half story frame Victorian residences.

94 Church Street

93 Church Street

95 Church Street

Church St.

$\mathscr{C}$HARLESTON'S economy suffered severe economic depression following the Revolution and myth would have it that no houses were built in the Victorian era for this reason. *99 Church* is one of the lovely classic Victorian houses, built in 1910, which belays that myth. Invention of the cotton gin was a major force in helping Charleston regain its prosperity. Church Street is a wonderful example of pre-revolutionary and Victorian houses delightfully and indiscriminately interspersed.

The double tenement at *143-145 Church* was constructed about 1740 by Alexander Peronneau, a Huguenot merchant. The basement of the structure is brick, the upper parts of Bermuda Stone. It was renovated and converted into a single residence in 1928 by Mrs. R. Goodwyn Rhett.

97 Church is another example of the two and one-half story Victorian residences built around 1910.

96 Church was built in 1760 by William Hall for Ann Peacock, a wealthy widow from St. George's Parish, Dorchester. The front portion of the house is a classic example of the Charleston Single House design. It is built on part of lot #37 of the original "Grand Modell" for Charleston.

99 Church Street

145 Church Street

97 Church Street

96 Church Street

132 Church Street

Legare St.

*L*EGARE Street was once called Johnson's Street for Sir Nathaniel Johnson, Governor of the Province from 1703 to 1709. The name was changed to Legare after Solomon Legaré, a prosperous Huguenot (French) silversmith and owner of large tracts of real estate at Legare and Tradd Streets.

8 Legare, built in 1857, is an example of the highly popular Italianate style of architecture popular during this period. This house was once the home of Burnet Rhett Maybank, mayor, governor and U.S. senator.

10 Legare was built in 1857 by Edward North Thurston. Its grand entrance and impressive lanterns mark the home of an important personage of the time. The arched door and recessed doorway were also popular during that period. It is thought that popular contractor Patrick O'Donnell built both *8 and 10 Legare*.

The home at *26 Legare* is of Colonial Revival style and had a columned portico before being remodeled in the Georgian style in 1937 by owner T. Wilbur Thornhill, an oil broker. Its entry features a fanlight window, a design borrowed from Georgian England and existing in many of Charleston's fine homes today.

5 Legare Street

8 Legare Street

10 Legare Street

10 Legare Street

26 Legare Street

Legare St.

*T*WENTY-TWO *Legare* features fine Georgian woodwork throughout its two and one-half story wooden construction. It was the city residence of planter Charles Elliott in 1764. Elliott's son-in-law, Col. William Washington, was related to President George Washington.

The house at *14 Legare* is a three and one-half story Adamesque brick home with a high basement. It was built in 1800 by Francis Simmons, a John's Island planter. Simmons lived in the house and his wife lived at 131 Tradd Street, where he left her on their wedding day. Their relationship was described as "casual though friendly." The "Pineapple" gates, actually crafted after pine cones, were added by planter and merchant George Edwards after 1816.

The Rev. Paul Trapier Gervais built the home at *29 Legare* in 1835, re-using the first floor of a brick house built there before 1788. Gervais was the rector of St. John's Episcopal Church on John's Island and published a pamphlet opposing secession.

31 Legare was built by Mrs. William Heyward in 1789 in the Adamesque style. It has a lovely second floor drawing room with a Palladian window in the curving south bay. Mrs. Heyward was the sister-in-law of Thomas Heyward, signer of the Declaration of Independence, and a successful rice planter in her own right. The house is said to be haunted by the ghost of her son who fatally shot himself in a hunting accident. It is claimed that he appeared to his sister in the library of the home at the instant of his death. He has put in few appearances since.

22 Legare Street

14 Legare Street

29 Legare Street

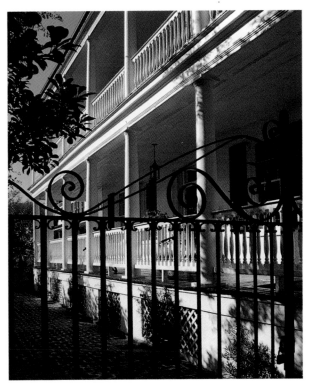

19 Legare Street

31 Legare Street

Legare St.

*S*word Gates House at *32 Legare* was built in the early 1800's by German merchants Jacob E.A. Steinmetz and Paul Emil Lorent. The dwelling is of frame and masonry construction linked by a frame addition. A romantic tale tells of the elopement of Maria Whaley, 15-year-old daughter of a wealthy planter, and George F. Morris, a New York "Yankee" during the period the home was used as an antebellum school for girls. It is said that Miss Whaley scaled the wall to marry Mr. Morris without her parents' permission. The sword gates, made a decade earlier as part of two sets for the Guard House at Broad and Meeting Streets, were added by George Hopley, British consul, in 1849. The avenue of magnolias was planted by Robert Adger in the mid-1800's. The lovely fences surrounding most of Charleston's dwellings served a duel purpose. In addition to adding beauty and privacy for the residents, they also served to keep some in. Servants in bondage, slaves, could not be allowed undue freedom. Fences with discreetly locked gates allowed the masters to keep tabs on these domestic laborers.

The home at *36 Legare* has been modernized. The first floor piazza has been enclosed to form rooms and a new entrance. Most of the second floor has been screened.

36 Legare St.

32 Legare St.

32 Legare St.

Tradd St.

TRADD Street was either named for Richard Tradd who built his home there in 1696 at the northeast corner of Tradd and East Bay, or for his son, Robert. The home at *38 Tradd* is a quaint two and one-half story, stuccoed brick built between 1718 and 1722 by John Bullock or his widow, Mary. This home became the studio and residence of artist Elizabeth O'Neill Verner after 1838.

Number *40 Tradd* was also built by Bullock or his widow in 1718. Col. Robert Brewton, son-in-law of Bullock, sold the house in 1752 to Daniel Badger.

54 Tradd, a three and one-half story stuccoed brick house built around 1740, subsequently belonged to Peter Bacot, President Washington's Charleston Postmaster.

56 Tradd was erected by George Ducat (Ducatt), a ship-builder, in 1739. The house is constructed of brick and Bermuda stone and was "Adamized" in 1800.

James Vanderhorst built the home at *46 Tradd* in 1770. The three story stuccoed brick house has also been the home of the well known artist Alfred Hutty. The entry bears a classic example of the Georgian semi-circular window known as a fanlight.

52 Tradd Street

3 Tradd Street

29 Tradd Street

38 · 40 · 42 Tradd Street

56 · 54 Tradd Street

46 Tradd Street

Tradd St.

A Tory (British sympathizer) built the house at *106 Tradd* before 1772. He was Col. John Stuart, Royal Commissioner of Indian Affairs. Stuart's properties were confiscated by patriots after the Revolution. The home is a three and one-half story wood construction with a hipped roof and a "captain's walk." A later owner added the two story octagonal wing and the piazza.

172 Tradd was built by Alexander Hext Chisolm, owner of Chisolm's Rice Mill, in 1836. It is a fine example of Greek Revival architecture. The huge portico uses the Corinthian order from the Choragic Movement of Lysicrates, with the original marble imitated in hand-carved wood. The interior has a gracefully curving staircase, a mark of class and distinction in that era. Lacy ironwork gates have been popular since Colonial times.

70 Tradd, a large single house, was built by Judge Robert Pringle in 1774 and still bears the placque stating his name and date of construction. Pringle, a wealthy merchant from Scotland, willed the home to his son John Julius Pringle, who served as Attorney General of South Carolina for 16 years and District Attorney for the state under President Washington.

60 Tradd, a three and one-half story stuccoed brick single house, was built in 1732 by ship builder George Ducat for his daughter Margaret on her marriage to Dr. William Cleland of Crail, Scotland.

106 Tradd Street

172 Tradd Street

70 Tradd Street

172 Tradd Street

60 Tradd Street

Meeting St.

*I*N the grand plan for Charleston, laid out by Lord Shaftesbury in 1672, Meeting Street was supposed to have been the city's main artery and was to have a meeting house and a park. King Street, due to its location, became the city's highway instead. The street did get the meeting house for which it was named, however, White Meeting House of the Independents or Congregationalists.

The Italianate style dwelling at *1 Meeting* is a three story brick construction built on a high brick basement. It was constructed in 1846 for George Robertson, a cotton broker.

Josiah Smith, a prosperous merchant, commissioned the building of *7 Meeting* sometime before 1788. A two and one-half story wood structure on a high brick foundation, the house features a hipped roof and cupola. The walls are insulated with brick between the framing timbers. The simple pediment fronting the street is accented with a round window. A semi-circular porch graces the street side. Smith was arrested and exiled to St. Augustine by the British in 1780. After the Revolution he returned and once again became a successful merchant and banker. He sold the house to Wilson Glover in 1800.

7 Meeting Street

7 Meeting Street

1 Meeting Street

1 Meeting Street

Meeting St.

THE home at *2 Meeting* is marked by romantic Queen Anne architecture. The story is told that wealthy banker George W. Williams placed $75,000 on a satin pillow as a wedding gift for his daughter Martha and Waring P. Carrington in 1890. The young couple used the money to build this charming house. For their fifth wedding anniversary, the Carrington's were given tiffany windows. Carrington, wealthy in his own right, had a thriving jewelry business on King Street. The wrought iron fence which shields the home from the street is breached by an unusual gate with an arching curve overhead accented with a gas lantern. Today, the house is enjoyed by many as a romantic Bed and Breakfast.

The Tucker-Ladson house at *8 Meeting* shows evidence of several owners' tastes. The rear part of the house is oldest, built in 1783 by Capt. Thomas Tucker, a merchant, shopowner and political and military leader in the Revolution. Abraham Crouch added the Adamesque details after purchasing the house in 1806. James Henry Ladson, a factor and planter, bought the house in 1821, adding the front portion and giving it the appearance of a three story Regency period town house. Finely detailed wrought and cast iron work mark the elevated piazzas.

2 Meeting Street

8 Meeting Street

8 Meeting Street

Meeting St.

THE Calhoun Mansion at *16 Meeting* is considered to be one of the most important Victorian mansions on the Eastern Seaboard. It was completed in 1876 by George W. Williams, a wealthy banker and merchant. The mansion has about 35 rooms and 24,000 square feet of floor space (including the attic) and is the largest building in the city constructed as a single residence. The house features 14 foot ceilings, elaborate plaster and woodwork and a stairwell that ascends to a 75 foot high domed ceiling. The ballroom has a covered glass skylight 45 feet high. Upon Williams' death, the property went to his son-in-law, Patrick Calhoun, a grandson of the "Great Nullifier," John C. Calhoun. After WWI, the mansion served as a hotel known as the Calhoun Mansion. Today it is a museum.

The large stuccoed brick house at *11 Meeting* was built in the Italianate style by William C. Courtney in 1855. It occupies the middle of Town Lot No. 117 of the Grand Modell, including an enlarged rear section created when Josiah Smith filled the marshlands between Meeting and King Streets.

The large, somewhat unusual semicircular piazza of *15 Meeting* was added to this 1770 home by then owner George W. Williams, Jr., according to historical legend, in order to accommodate all the children of the Charleston Orphan House for ice cream socials. The house was constructed by John Edwards with cypress boards cut and beveled to resemble the impressive character of stone block.

16 Meeting Street

15 Meeting Street

11 Meeting Street

Meeting St.

Thirty Meeting, as legend would have it, offered its broad chimney as a hiding place for German Hessian troops who deserted during the Redcoat Roundup following the Revolutionary War. The house was completed by Col. Isaac Motte, a plantation owner and French Huguenot revolutionary in 1770. It is typical of early Georgian architecture adapted to Charleston's climate and lifestyle by the addition of three broad piazzas running the entire length of the house.

The house at *23 Meeting* predates Motte's house by 19 years. It is a three and one-half story single house believed to have been built in 1750 by Albert Detmar.

18 Meeting's origins are a bit clouded. It was probably built by Nathaniel Heyward before 1803 and sold to his half brother Thomas Heyward, signer of the Declaration of Independence, in 1803. It is of single house style with Adamesque details in the interior. The second floor has a secret room which may have been a wine closet. In 1858, the house was the home of James Adger, operator of the first coastal steamship line in the U.S.

Regency was the style chosen for *26 Meeting*. The home was built in 1822 by William Mason Smith, son of Rt. Rev. Robert Smith, South Carolina's first Episcopal bishop. The three levels of piazzas, having the "correct" sequence of orders: Doric, Ionic and Corinthian, are masked from the street by a screen of masonry with windows.

30 Meeting Street

23 Meeting Street

26 Meeting Street

18 Meeting Street

22 Meeting Street

21 Meeting Street

Meeting St.

$\mathcal{J}$T seems that the house at *34 Meeting* had the unfortunate habit of dropping bits of its facade on unsuspecting people throughout its early years. Francis Kinloch Huger, remembered for his unsuccessful attempt to rescue Lafayette from the Castle of Olmutz, was nearly killed when a bit of masonry ornamentation fell and fractured his skull on the front steps in 1794. An English visitor wasn't as lucky. Part of the repaired parapet fell during the earthquake of 1886 and he was killed. Ripe with history, the house was the residence of South Carolina's last Royal Governor - who had to sneak away in the night to save his life from Revolutionaries. Bombardments by Federal troops shook the home in 1863-65 and Federal troops looted and vandalized it in 1865. Owned by Charlton DeSaussure, Sr., the home continues to stand proudly, no longer dropping its decorative trim.

The home at *31 Meeting* was built in 1792 by Major James Ladson, a revolutionary officer, state representative and delegate to the South Carolina Convention to ratify the Federal Constitution. The entrance was changed from Ladson Street to the piazza on Meeting by E.M. Beach. The fountain, a duplicate of one in the Kaiserhoff Garden at Bad Nauheim, Germany, was added by the wife of Christopher P. Poppenheim, a planter and merchant who acquired the property in 1877.

34 Meeting Street

34 Meeting Street

31 Meeting Street

37 Meeting Street

Meeting St.

*T*HE house at *37 Meeting* is often referred to as "Double Breasted" or the "Bosoms" house. The large curving bays were added after 1809. The house has seen its share of Charleston's colorful history. During the Revolution it was confiscated and ransacked by the British and, in the Civil War, it served as headquarters for dashing Confederate commander Gen. Pierre G.T. Beauregard for a time. There's even a legend that pirate treasure is buried on the property - guarded by the ghost of an unfortunate pirate who tried to sneak back and retrieve the loot one dark night.

36 Meeting hides an elegant 18th century house with fine Georgian interior featured behind a mid-19th century Greek Revival parapet.

The windows in the mansard roof of *38 Meeting* probably led to either the children's or servants' quarters. The children's rooms were usually on the third floor while the servants were housed in either the kitchen building or separate buildings on the back of the lot.

The tall stuccoed brick house at *35 Meeting* is believed to have been built in 1720 by the first Lieutenant Governor of South Carolina, William Bull. His son William was the first native South Carolinian to receive a medical degree and like his father also served as Lieutenant Governor.

36 Meeting Street

38 Meeting Street

38 Meeting Street

35 Meeting Street

Meeting St.

ONE of the finest examples of Federal architecture in America, *51 Meeting* was built in 1808 by Nathaniel Russell, a Rhode Island merchant who amassed a fortune in Charleston. The mansion features an octagonal bay, a wrought iron balcony and a balustraded parapet. Perhaps its most impressive feature is the free flying staircase that rises three floors without visible means of support. The house and gardens are maintained by Historic Charleston Foundation and guided tours are conducted daily.

39 Meeting was built in 1767 as St. Michael's rectory. Construction is credited to a Mr. Miller and John Fullerton, master builders responsible for many of Charleston's fine homes.

The gardens of fruit and vegetables next to *47 Meeting* were the pride and joy of Edward Barnwell, who won several silver cups for his efforts. Barnwell, a factor and planter, was equally proud of his 17 children. It is said that Barnwell added on to the rear of the house several times to accommodate his remarkable family.

51 Meeting Street

51 Meeting Street

51 Meeting Street

39 Meeting Street

47 Meeting Street

Meeting St.

THE three story frame house of Andrew Hasell at *64 Meeting* was one of the last built on the street in the late 1700's. It features one of Charleston's classically elegant entry doors which leads to a two story piazza overlooking a walled garden.

Timothy Ford, an attorney from New Jersey, built the three and one-half story brick house with raised basement at *54 Meeting* in 1800. It still contains some of the finest Adamesque interior details in all of Charleston as well as a lovely garden.

60 Meeting was built as a double tenement apartment building in 1771. The eastern half is 64 Tradd Street. The building was remodeled in high Victorian style by Bertram Kramer, a bridge and wharf builder and general contractor, in 1893.

59 Meeting is a fine Georgian double house. Built in 1751 by a wealthy planter, William Branford, it is noted for fine cedar paneling and elaborate mantels. The double piazzas held up by graceful columns were built in 1830 by Brandford's grandson, Elias Horry, President of the South Carolina Railroad and the College of Charleston. The lower portico is finely detailed and the upper level is protected by fine ironwork.

64 Meeting Street

54 Meeting Street

54 Meeting Street

60 Meeting Street

59 Meeting Street

Meeting St.

SIXTY-EIGHT Meeting has served many purposes. The house was built in 1810 by John Cordes Prioleau, a factor and planter. It was his house slave who warned his master of a plot by a free black man to instigate a slave uprising in the city. Because of this information thirty-four people were hanged and the revolt was aborted. Later, from 1855-1862 the home was used as a school by Madame Rosalie Acelie Tongo. In 1886, Dr. Charles U. Shepard took up residence, using a small garden building as a laboratory for analytical chemistry. Dr. Shepard was also famous for his farm at Summerville where he grew tea commercially and for experimentation.

The three and one-half story home at *69 Meeting* was also the residence of a physician. Dr. John Ernest Poyas, Jr. constructed this home between 1796 and 1800. The home has lovely Adamesque interiors.

Manigault is one of the oldest names in Charleston history. Brothers Pierre and Gabriel arrived around 1695, fleeing religious persecution in France. Pierre's son, Gabriel, established the family name in Charleston through mercantile interests and his son, Gabriel, a talented amateur architect, continued the tradition. Young Gabriel designed *350 Meeting* for his brother Joseph in 1803. The house follows the elegance and simplicity associated with the designs of Robert Adam, a noted Scottish architect, creator of the Adamesque style. Owned by The Charleston Museum, the house is open to the public.

350 Meeting Street

69 Meeting Street

68 Meeting Street

Broad St.

*I*N Charleston's Grand Modell, Broad Street was just that, the broadest street. 92 Broad is referred to as Dr. David Ramsay's House. A physician and historian, Ramsay was deeply involved in the politics of the day, served as a war surgeon, and later wrote several volumes on Charleston, South Carolina and American history. He was murdered by a deranged patient in 1815.

Peter Bocquet, Jr., a merchant and planter, built the three and one-half story stuccoed brick home at 95 Broad on land gifted to him by his father in 1770. Bocquet owned several plantations and was active in the Revolution. The exterior of the house has been altered but the door on the left side dates from the Regency period, c. 1815-25. The wrought iron balcony is also considered to be original.

The home at 114 Broad was built by planter Ralph Izard in 1790 but remained unfinshed until 1829 when it was purchased by Col. Thomas Pickney Jr . Gen. Pierre G.T. Beauregard, used the house for headquarters for five months in 1863 during which time Confederate President Jefferson Davis was an honored guest.

95 Broad Street

92 Broad Street

114 Broad Street

Broad St.

ALTHOUGH built in 1760 by James Laurens, the house at *117 Broad* is referred to as the Edward Rutledge House. Rutledge, a signer of the Declaration of Independence, purchased the house from the Laurens estate in 1788. An attorney, Rutledge served as Governor of South Carolina in 1798. The house was Victorianized after 1885 by Capt. Frederick Wagener, a horse breeder and racer, and the exterior remodeled in the Colonial Revival style by Dr. Josiah Smith, after 1935.

The John Rutledge House Inn at *116 Broad Street* was built in 1763 for his bride, Elizabeth Grimke. Rutledge was a member of the South Carolina Assembly, the Stamp Act Congress and the Continental Congress. John Rutledge was co-author and signer of the U.S. Constitution. He was governor of the state from 1779-83, and an Associate and Chief Justice of the Supreme Court. In 1853, Thomas Norman Gadsten, a real estate broker and slave trader, bought and remodeled the house. He added the terra cotta window cornices and the wrought iron balconies. The ironwork is attributed to Christopher Werner and incorporates two of his favorite motifs: the palmetto tree of South Carolina and the United States eagle. The work is a combination of wrought and cast iron.

The house at *181 Broad* presents its charming facade from behind a classic stuccoed brick and wrought iron fence. Part of the lower piazza has been enclosed and converted into living space.

117 Broad Street

181 Broad Street

116 Broad Street

116 Broad Street

Charleston

7 Limehouse St.

EARLY every one of Charleston's streets and thoroughfares is rich in history. So many of Charleston's buildings have withstood wars, depression, hostile occupation and nature's worst in the form of fires, floods, earthquakes and hurricanes. Limehouse Street was named for the Limehouse family, through whose land the street was cut.

7 Limehouse, a small two and one half story brick home, is believed to have been built in 1830 by Robert Limehouse.

9 Limehouse was built by William Pinckney Shingler, a planter and cotton broker, in 1856. Financial problems forced him to sell the house almost immediately. By 1858, however, he had regained his fortune and built number 10 in a similar style.

Chalmers Street, once known as Chalmers Alley, was named for Dr. Lionel Chalmers, an eminent Scottish physician and scientist who did important work on tetanus and fevers.

John Breton built the Pink House, as it became known, at *17 Chalmers* in 1712. The tiny structure is believed to have been a tavern in Colonial days. It is constructed of Bermuda stone, a coral limestone imported in blocks from Bermuda. The building's gambrel roof is one of only a few surviving in Charleston.

17 Chalmers St.

9 Limehouse St.

Charleston

ORANGE Street was created along the eastern boundary of the Orange Garden, a park devoted to concerts under the fragrant shade of an orange grove. Alexander Petrie divided the property on the west side of the street into building lots for the nation's first racially integrated "subdivision." One of the lots was sold at public auction to "Amy, a free woman of color."

7 Orange was built on part of the site of the original orange grove by Col. Charles Pickney in 1769. Known as The Rivers House, this home had a number of owners before being acquired by M. Rutledge Rivers, a lawyer, educator and civic leader.

9 Orange is part of a three and one-half story double frame tenement built in 1770. This building was constructed when the term tenement meant a building with multiple dwellings and, with its gracious beauty, belays the more derogatory current meaning of the word.

9 Orange Street

3 Orange Street

7 Orange Street

7 Orange Street

Charleston

BARRE Street (pronounced Barry) was surveyed in 1770 and is named in honor of Isaac Barre, a sponsor of the cause against "taxation without representation." The Gov. Thomas Bennett House at *69 Barre* was built by Thomas Bennett, Jr., member of the S.C. House of Representatives, Speaker of the House, member of the Senate and Governor of South Carolina 1820-22. Built in 1825, the home originally looked out on Bennett's rice plantation, saw mills and mill ponds.

Adger's Wharf, one of several streets made by filling low lands, began its history as a "low water lot," exposed only at low tide. The land was filled to expand the ever growing city. In the 1830's and 40's, James Adger used the wharfs as the southern terminus of the first steamship line between Charleston and New York. This lucrative venture allegedly made him the richest man in South Carolina. In later years, large brick buildings lined the streets and were used as cotton warehouses and brokers' offices. At the end of port activity, the wharfs were abandoned and the buildings converted to residences and offices.

Lowndes Grove at *266 St. Margaret Street* was originally a plantation house built in 1786 by George Abbot Hall to replace one on another part of the property burned by British troops during the Revolution. Located on the Ashley River and beautifully landscaped by live oaks, "The Grove" was once the site of a duel between two generals, both of whom wished to be in charge of South Carolina troops.

69 Barre Street

69 Barre Street

35 N. Adger's Wharf

266 St. Margaret Street

Charleston

*L*ENWOOD Boulevard was named in honor of Gen. Leonard Wood, a U.S. Army commander in Charleston during World War I. Lenwood Boulevard was created as part of the Murray Boulevard development in the early 20th century and is graced with many lovely homes from that period.

Queen Street is one of the original streets in the Grand Modell. First called Dock Street for a boat dock at its swampy end, the street was renamed Queen for Caroline of Ansbach, the consort of George II. *22-28 Queen* is a notable row of three and one-half story stuccoed brick tenements built in the 1790's by the family of William Johnson, Associate Justice of the U.S. Supreme Court.

Bull Street was named for William Bull, a native South Carolinian who was the last to fill the Royally-appointed office of Lieutenant Governor.

The William Blacklock House, at *18 Bull*, was built in 1800 and is one of the nation's finest examples of Adamesque architecture. The house is constructed of Charleston grey brick, accented by stone trim. A double flight of iron railed stairs leads to the entry surrounded by sidelights and a fanlight with delicate traceries. The interior features excellent Adamesque woodwork and plasterwork and a graceful circular stair under an unusual vaulted ceiling. It is suggested that Gabriel Manigault, who served with Blacklock on the building committee for the bank, which is now City Hall, designed the house.

46 Lenwood Boulevard

30 · 28 · 26 · 24 · 22 Queen Street

18 Bull Street

Charleston

ALHOUN Street is named for John C. Calhoun, the "Great Nullifier." *Number 268*, a large frame house in the Greek Revival style, was built between 1838 and 1846 by Edward Sebring, president of the State Bank of South Carolina.

Ashley Avenue began as Lynch Street, named for Thomas Lynch. It was lengthened and changed names several times before becoming Ashley in 1897. The outstanding Greek Revival mansion at *178 Ashley* was built in 1850 by John Hume Lucas, a wealthy planter. It is a two-storied wood structure on a rusticated masonry basement. The columns on the front portico and the giant columns of the piazza have Tower of the Winds capitals, a form of Greek Cornithian.

The buildings at *2, 4 and 6 St. Michael's Alley* are classic examples of British style house placement. Each rests against the sidewalk and crowds against its neighbor, with blank wall sides.

Elizabeth Street was named for Elizabeth Wragg, daughter of Joseph Wragg and mother of architect Gabriel Manigault. The Aiken-Rhett House, at *48 Elizabeth Street*, was built by John Robinson in 1817 as a simple double house. Governor William Aiken acquired the property in 1832 and remodeled the house in Greek Revival Style to the expansive 23 rooms seen today. Confederate General Beauregard used the house as his headquarters during the bombardment of Charleston and President Jefferson Davis was the guest of honor at a dinner when he visited in November, 1863. Owned by The Charleston Museum, the house is open to the public.

268 Calhoun Street

6 · 4 · 2 St. Michael's Alley

178 Ashley Avenue

48 Elizabeth Street

Charleston

IBBES Street is named for William Gibbes, who assisted in the filling of marshlands north of South Bay (South Battery) in the first half of the 1700's. The Parker-Drayton House at *6 Gibbes* was built in 1806 by Isaac Parker, a planter in St. Thomas and St. Denis Parish and a brickyard owner. Col. William Drayton remodeled it in the Regency style with winnings from the East Bay Lottery in 1820.

Ladson Street is named for Lt. Gov. James Ladson, who built the wooden house at the corner of Meeting and Ladson in 1791. The street is older than its name, however, being cut through Lt. Gov. William Bull's land to create a lot for his son-in-law, John Drayton.

Beaufain Street originally followed the north line of the Grand Modell for Charles Town. It was named for Hector Berenger de Beaufain, a French Huguenot and prominent Charleston citizen. *108 Beaufain* was built between 1840 and 1842 by sawmill owner John Steinmeyer. The home features shiplap siding scored to resemble stone blocks and an interior combining both Greek Revival features from the 1840's and Victorian features from the 1870's.

The tall three and one-half story brick single house at *110 Beaufain* was built in 1852 by a merchant, Robert Shands Smith.

Elliott Street was laid out in 1683 and came by its present name for the family who owned Elliott's Bridge (wharf) and much of the street's real estate. *16 and 18 Elliott* were built by William Mills, a tailor and philanthropist, in 1802, as tenements. He left number 16 to his daughter and number 18 to his son.

6 Gibbes Street

9 Ladson Street

108 Beaufain Street

110 Beaufain Street

16 · 18 Elliott Street

Rutledge Ave.

RUTLEDGE Avenue was named for John Rutledge, President and Governor of South Carolina, as well as a delegate to the Continental Congress and U.S. Constitutional Convention. The home at *22 Rutledge* was built in 1902 in an early 20th century interpretation of Renaissance style, popular at the South Carolina Inter-State and West Indian Exposition held in Charleston in 1901-02.

40 Rutledge was built by Albert W. Todd, an architect, in 1903. Of Colonial Revival style, woodwork from Belvedere Plantation on Charleston Neck was installed in the 1920's.

Another example of Colonial Revival style architecture, *64 Rutledge* was built in 1908 by George Harper.

The exact history of *74 Rutledge* has never been determined. It may have been built before 1783 by Isaac Child Harleston, a member of the First Provincial Congress, or by Maj. Peter Bocquet, a Revolutionary politician and officer, between 1783 and 1793. There is also the belief that it was built by John Mathews, Governor of South Carolina, between 1796 and 1802. Most of the interior is Adamesque, dating the house to the 1800's but some Georgian features point to the possibility of earlier construction.

64 Rutledge Avenue

22 Rutledge Avenue

40 Rutledge Avenue

74 Rutledge Avenue

Rutledge Ave.

*T*HE home at *94 Rutledge* was built by Isaac Jenkins Mikell, a wealthy Edisto Island planter, for his third wife. The impressive Italianate villa style home features Jupiter or ram's head capitals on its massive pillars. The interior of this stately home is graced with a curving staircase and ornate plasterwork, much in demand at the time. In 1857, the house was described as "one of the most ambitious of the private dwellings in Charleston." In 1866, after real estate values collapsed, the home was sold to merchant Edward Willis. It was also home to Mayor John Ficken and served as the Charleston County Free Library from 1935 to 1960.

Ashley Hall School at *172 Rutledge* was built in 1816 by Patrick Duncan in the Regency villa style. James R. Pringle, speaker of the South Carolina House and customs collector, purchased the home in 1838. Later it belonged to George A. Trenholm, owner of Civil War blockade running ships and Confederate Secretary of the Treasury. From 1870 to 1907, it was the home of German Consul Charles O. Witte. In 1909, Miss Mary Vardrine McBee opened Ashley Hall School in the building.

94 Rutledge Avenue

94 Rutledge Avenue

172 Rutledge Avenue

King St.

KING Street, part of Charles Town's Grand Modell, was named, of course, for England's monarch. During Charles Town's early days it was the main highway in and out of the settlement, traversing a high ridge between the marshy lowlands of the peninsula.

The three and one-half story stuccoed brick home at *21 King* was built for Patrick O'Donnell in 1856-57 and is one of the most elaborate Italianate style homes in the city. The house was nicknamed "O'Donnell's Folly" because it took so long to build that his prospective bride tired of waiting and married another. O'Donnell lived alone in the large house, dying a bachelor. O'Donnell's bad luck followed beyond the grave as well. He left his estate to be administered by Father Tom Burke for the poor of his native Galway. Burke made off with most of the money.

Built between 1765 and 1769, The Miles Brewton House, at *27 King* is so lovely that not one, but two, invading armies used it as headquarters. The High Georgian double house was first used by the British during their occupation of the city in the Revolutionary War, and again by Union Generals after the surrender of Charleston in the Civil War.

21 King Street

21 King Street

27 King Street

27 King Street

46 King Street

King St.

JOHN McKee's two and one-half story brick house is a classic example of the "Single House" style of architecture. McKee, a brick-mason, had the house at *44 King* built in 1796.

Florist Walter Webb would be pleased with the gardens which still adorn his house at *46 King*. Webb laid out the original gardens after building the two story brick house in 1851. The front entry was moved after an automobile crashed into the home in the 1930's.

The home at *47 King* features the symmetrical layout so much favored by Charleston residents throughout the years.

Most of the history of *54 King* is lost but it is believed the home was built in 1768.

The thick walls and low ceilings of *75 King* point to the supposition that this house was built prior to 1739. It's ownership was credited to William Elliott.

46 King Street

47 King Street

44 King Street

75 King Street

44 King Street

54 King Street

54 King Street

East Battery

East Bay Street traverses most of the eastern side of the Charleston peninsula before joining with East Battery and then West Battery to travel past White Point Gardens and on up the western tip to Chisolm Street. East Battery, named for cannons deployed there during the War of 1812, was constructed next to a continuously refortified seawall protecting the southern tip of the peninsula.

Thomas A. Coffin built the three story stuccoed brick mansion at *1 East Battery* in about 1850. He sold it to Louis deSaussure in 1858 and the house is still referred to as the deSaussure House. Having one of the finest locations in Charleston, the home has seen history in the making.

The Victorian mansion at *25 East Battery* was built for Charles H. Drayton in 1885. Drayton made his fortune mining phosphate deposits for fertilizer on his family plantation on the Ashley River. The home was originally constructed of white brick with black exposed mortar and reflected Medieval European and Chinese architectural styles. It has since been stuccoed.

East Battery

25 East Battery

1 East Battery

East Battery

13 East Battery

*N*UMBER *9 East Battery* was the first large house to be built on that portion of the street which was exposed to the devastating forces of hurricane winds. It was completed in 1838 for Robert William Roper, a planter. The massive pillars fronting the home look a bit too grand at close range but must have impressed Roper's contemporaries as they traveled the Ashley River. The large rope molding surrounding the entry door was probably also a bit of Roper's design - a play upon his name, a device used in English heraldry.

The 1845 home William Ravenel, a rich shipping merchant, built at *13 East Battery* has been remodeled by the hand of Mother Nature. The arcaded base of the front portico is all that remains of huge Tower of the Winds columns which crashed earthward in the 1886 earthquake. A hurricane in the 1950's uncovered one of the huge capitals, apparently buried deeply in the ground by the force of its fall. The large house was constructed on a very narrow lot by running the porte-cochere (an entrance for vehicles) under the drawing room.

When it was built in 1920 for Julius M. Visanka, the home at *19 East Battery* was one of the most expensive in Charleston. It stands in the site of Lyttelton's Bastion, a fort built in 1757.

9 East Battery

17 East Battery

19 East Battery

East Battery

5 East Battery

T HE earthquake of 1886 severely damaged the three story stuccoed brick home at *5 East Battery* which had been built between 1847-49 for John Ravenel, a Huguenot planter and merchant. Following the home's original Italianate style, Elias Horry Frost, Ravenel's son-in-law, restored the building and added Victorian Italianate features popular at the time.

The Edmondston-Alston House at *21 East Battery* was built in 1825 by Charles Edmondston, a native of the Shetland Islands, and a local wharf owner and merchant. Charles Alston bought the house in 1838 and added such Greek Revival features as the third level piazza and the roof parapet with his family's coat of arms. The parapet and balcony were destroyed during the 1886 earthquake and had to be replaced. After Charleston's surrender during the Civil War, the home was occupied by Union Maj. Gen. Rufus Saxton. Charles Alston's daughter, Susan Pringle Alston, was the last of his family to live in the home, passing away in 1921. Today, the Edmonston-Alston House is a museum owned by the Middleton Place Foundation.

21 East Battery

21 East Battery

East Battery

NUMBER 2 Water Street is on the corner of Water and East Bay streets. It was built by Nathaniel Ingraham, a merchant, in 1810-12 and later belonged to Confederate historian Edward L. Wells.

The large home at *31 East Battery* features a center front bay which relieves its otherwise austere appearance.

The Porcher-Simonds House at *29 East Battery* was built in 1856 for Francis J. Porcher, a cotton broker and, after the Civil War, president of the Atlantic Phosphate Company. The original house, was built in the Italianate style with a pedimented center pavilion and masked piazza. John C. Simonds, educated at Exeter and Yale, purchased the house in 1894 and remodeled it in the popular Italian Renaissance Revival style. The two front piazzas, one semi-circular and one square, were added at that time, as was a semi-oval wing on the south side. The interior was also redone, featuring dark oak and mahogany woodwork and two baronial staircases. Simonds, succeeding his father, was president of the First National Bank until he sold it in 1926, a precipitous move.

The home at *39 East Battery* has a two story piazza overlooking a walled garden.

2 Water Street

31 East Battery

39 East Battery

29 East Battery

29 East Battery

East Battery & East Bay

MOST of the construction on East Bay Street was accomplished after the Revolution although there are earlier houses. The east side of the street was fortified from invasion by Granville's Bastion on the South and Craven's Bastion on the north. The west side of the street attracted buildings which housed shops on the first floor and homes above.

The lovely three story stuccoed brick dwelling at *55 East Bay* was built in 1780 by Jonathan Simpson.

The three and one-half story Georgian style house at *43 East Battery* was built on part of Lot No. 1 of the Grand Modell, granted by the Lord Proprietors to Maurice Mathews and James Moore in 1682. The home was either built by Adam Daniel, prior to 1755, or shortly thereafter by George Sommers. The property remained in the Sommers family until the 1790's and the nearby curve in East Bay where it joins East Battery became known as Sommers' Corner.

45 East Battery is constructed on another part of Lot No. 1 conveyed to James Hartley in 1757. Hartley's house did not survive and William Somersall, his son-in-law, built the present dwelling sometime after the Revolution. Somersall was a prosperous merchant and planter originally from St. Kitt's. He served on the state convention to ratify the U.S. Constitution in 1788. The home eventually came into the possession of Wilmot G. DeSaussure, a Confederate general, who completely remodeled it.

75 East Bay

55 East Bay

43 East Battery

41 East Battery

45 East Battery

East Bay

*T*HE double building at *99-101 East Bay* was built after the devastating fire of 1740 which leveled most of Charleston's waterfront. It is part of what is now called Rainbow Row and was built by Othneil Beale who was in charge of strengthening the city's fortifications. The building was restored in the 1930's.

95 East Bay, also on Rainbow Row, is an example of Flemish gabled construction. It was probably built shortly after the great fire of 1740 but the builder is unknown. Charles Cotesworth Pinckney, who was a delegate to the U.S. Constitutional Convention in 1790, minister to France in 1796 and an unsuccessful Federalist candidate for President in 1800, 1804 and 1808, also owned the home.

Rainbow Row, which consists of 14 private homes numbering from 83 to 107, dates from 1740 when it served as Charleston's waterfront district. The houses, by owners' choice, are painted in a rainbow of colors. Most of the buildings were originally constructed as a combination business and residence.

107, the last home on Rainbow Row, was built in 1792 by John Blake using the wall of the building to the south to support his joists.

99 · 101 East Bay

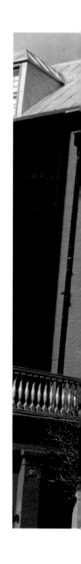

95 East Bay

Rainbow Row

East Bay

TAILOR and livery stable owner Benjamin Dupre built the two story wooden home on a high brick basement at *317 East Bay* between 1803 and 1805. The home features lovely Adamesque details throughout the interior.

The stately mansion at *631 East Bay* is called the Faber-Ward House. It was built around 1832 by Henry F. Faber. The architecture was copied from Andrea Palladio, a noted Italian designer of the 16th century. The stone arches which support the pillared piazza are each 15 feet tall. Joshua Ward, a wealthy and famous rice planter as well as South Carolina's Lieutenant Governor, purchased the home from Faber. No expense was spared in the construction of this home and materials such as Italian marble and mahogany imported from the tropics saw lavish usage. The house fell from grace when Union troops occupied the city, converting the mansion into a hotel for recently emancipated slaves. The hotel failed and the house again became a private residence for a while before being turned into apartments and sliding into a post World War II decline. Most of its neighboring mansions did not survive this era. Today only one remains, along with the sad shell of another. *631 East Bay* has been turned into an office building with three apartments. The house however, still stands as mute testimony to the era when Charleston was the Queen city of the South.

71 East Bay

73 East Bay

317 East Bay

631 East Bay